KT-462-427

THE ANCIENT
Chinese

Louise Spilsbury

WITHDRAWN

C334544469

Raintree is an imprint of Capstone Global Library Limited, a company incorporated in England and Wales having its registered office at 264 Banbury Road, Oxford, OX2 7DY – Registered company number: 6695582

www.raintree.co.uk
myorders@raintree.co.uk

Text © Capstone Global Library Limited 2021
The moral rights of the proprietor have been asserted.

All rights reserved. No part of this publication may be reproduced in any form or by any means (including photocopying or storing it in any medium by electronic means and whether or not transiently or incidentally to some other use of this publication) without the written permission of the copyright owner, except in accordance with the provisions of the Copyright, Designs and Patents Act 1988 or under the terms of a licence issued by the Copyright Licensing Agency, Barnard's Inn, 86 Fetter Lane, London, EC4A 1EN (www.cla.co.uk). Applications for the copyright owner's written permission should be addressed to the publisher.

Produced for Raintree by Calcium Creative Ltd
Edited by Sarah Eason and Jennifer Sanderson
Designed by Paul Myerscough and Jessica Moone
Media research by Rachel Blount
Original illustrations © Capstone Global Library Limited 2020
Production by Tori Abraham
Originated by Capstone Global Library Ltd
Printed and bound in India

978 1 4747 9773 3 (hardback)
978 1 4747 9774 0 (paperback)

British Library Cataloguing in Publication Data
A full catalogue record for this book is available from the British Library.

Acknowledgements
We would like to thank the following for permission to reproduce photographs: Cover: Shutterstock: Photosync; Inside: LACMA/www.lacma.org: Gift of Mr. and Mrs. Eric Lidow: p. 12; Gift of Mr. Ernest F. and Mrs. Mae R. Roberson: p. 19; Shutterstock: Aphotostory: p. 23; Beibaoke: p. 27; Hung Chung Chih: pp. 10-11, 15; Delpixel: p. 16; Elena Elisseeva: p. 32; Xidong Luo: p. 4; OBB APH: pp. 11t, 45; Sean Pavone: p. 39; Qingqing: p. 7; Tang Yan Song: p. 29; Trial: p. 14; Wikimedia Commons: pp. 5, 22; BabelStone: p. 26; Changsha: Hunan Provincial Museum: p. 35; Daderot: pp. 1, 24b, 24-25t, 34, 38; Deror_avi: p. 31; Drs2biz: p. 18; Editor at Large: pp. 8, 13; G41rn8: p. 43; Galopin: p. 20; John Hill: p. 21; Hispalois: p. 42; Wang Jie: p. 28; Engraving by J. June after Augustin Heckel/Wellcome Images: p. 17; Mountain at Shanghai Museum: pp. 8-9t; PericlesofAthens: p. 40; Gary L. Todd, Ph.D., Professor of History, Sias International University, Xinzheng, China: p. 36; Tomtom08: p. 6; Wellcome Images: p. 33; Yug: p. 30; Zcm11: p. 41.

Every effort has been made to contact copyright holders of material reproduced in this book. Any omissions will be rectified in subsequent printings if notice is given to the publisher.

All the internet addresses (URLs) given in this book were valid at the time of going to press. However, due to the dynamic nature of the internet, some addresses may have changed, or sites may have changed or ceased to exist since publication. While the author and publisher regret any inconvenience this may cause readers, no responsibility for any such changes can be accepted by either the author or the publisher.

CONTENTS

CHAPTER 1

China in ancient times

Chinese **civilization** is one of the oldest in the history of the world. From 4,000 years ago, or 2000 BC, China was ruled by a series of powerful **dynasties**, each named after the family of the ruling **emperor**. The name of the country itself – China – comes from the name of the Chinese Qin Dynasty, which is pronounced "Chin".

Around the river

Chinese **culture** grew from villages and settlements around the Yellow River, the second-largest river in China. For thousands of years, the Yellow River was known to the Chinese as the "mother river". China is surrounded by dry deserts and mountains, so people settled by the Yellow River because it could provide them with safe water to drink, wash and cook with. They could use it to water large fields of crops to feed growing populations. It was so important to the ancient Chinese that they often referred to it as simply *the* river.

THE YELLOW RIVER

The Yellow River was essential to the development of ancient Chinese civilization. It is called "Yellow River" because of the yellow colour of its muddy waters.

EMPEROR QIN
This is Qin Shi Huang, or Emperor Qin, the founder of the Qin Dynasty, from which the country of China took its name.

A united China

The first three dynasties to rule China were the Xia, Shang and Zhou dynasties. They ruled over the many early villages and farming communities around the Yellow River from 2070 BC to 256 BC.

After that time, there was a period when the area broke up into many small states that constantly battled for supreme control of the country. This was known as the Warring States period. It lasted until 221 BC, when the Qin kingdom conquered the armies of all the other states and took control. Their leader, Qin Shi Huang, united the country and became the emperor. Each dynasty had made an impact, but under Qin, and under the rule of the Han Dynasty that followed, China made great advances in science, art and technology.

Dynamic dynasties

The first dynasty to rule China was the Xia family. The Xia was the first dynasty because this family was the first to ensure power passed from father to son when their ruler died. The first king, Yu the Great, worked tirelessly to control the floods of the Yellow River, which frequently destroyed farmers' crops. He invented channels that diverted water from the river to farm fields further away.

The Shang and the Zhou dynasties

The Xia family ruled from 2070 BC to 1600 BC, when leaders of the Shang Dynasty overthrew them. The Xia leaders had become unpopular because they took so much money from the people to pay for grand building projects. The Shang lowered **taxes**, made advances, such as developing a system of writing, and carved beautiful objects in **jade**. The period of the Shang and the Zhou dynasties, which conquered the Shang in 1046, is generally known as the **Bronze** Age of China. This is because during that time, the Chinese developed a way of making bronze metal from copper and tin, and used it to make weapons, chariots and many other useful objects. Members of the Zhou Dynasty also taught people that their right to rule came from heaven. They introduced more religious **rituals**, which helped people identify as one country and culture.

THE GRAND CANAL
The Grand Canal was built during the Qin and other dynasties to transport grain from farms in the countryside to the cities.

The Qin and the Han dynasties

When Qin came to power in 221 BC, he ordered the walls that had divided the country to be broken down. Instead, he set up different districts, and built roads and canals to connect the different regions. He introduced systems of weights and measures to encourage trade. However, he was unpopular because he took high taxes from people to pay for projects such as a magnificent **tomb** for himself.

During the Han Dynasty that followed, from 206 BC to AD 222, art and science were encouraged and China was established as one of the most incredible cultures in world history.

USING BRONZE

In ancient China, bronze was used to make pots and containers that were decorated with religious **symbols** and used in rituals.

Examining evidence

We can unravel the secrets of a past culture from the writings they leave behind, but with ancient civilizations such as China, some written records may have been lost or rotted away over time. We can learn about how these people lived and who they were by examining other kinds of evidence too.

Digging up the past

Sometimes, people find remains of the past that are large and easily seen, such as sections of the Grand Canal built long ago, which tell us how important travel and trade were to the ancient Chinese. At other times, archaeologists who study ancient cultures must seek clues that may be hidden underground. They take photographs from the sky to locate places where the ground has been disturbed, hoping to find burial sites or the remains of ancient settlements where they can find **artefacts** from the past. Artefacts are pots, weapons and other items that can tell us about past lives. Sometimes, builders or farmers find artefacts by accident when they are digging up an area of land.

SKILLED POTTERS

This pitcher was used for storing and boiling liquid. Its carefully crafted shape shows us that the ancient Chinese were skilled at making pottery.

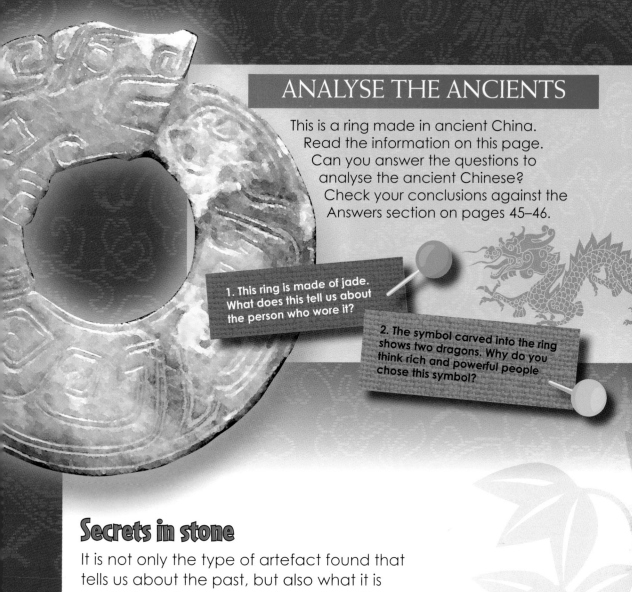

This is a ring made in ancient China. Read the information on this page. Can you answer the questions to analyse the ancient Chinese? Check your conclusions against the Answers section on pages 45–46.

1. This ring is made of jade. What does this tell us about the person who wore it?

2. The symbol carved into the ring shows two dragons. Why do you think rich and powerful people chose this symbol?

Secrets in stone

It is not only the type of artefact found that tells us about the past, but also what it is made from. For example, in ancient China, jade was a precious and rare stone that was very difficult and time-consuming to carve. It was often made into objects decorated with **mythical** creatures such as dragons, which were symbols of power and strength. So, if archaeologists find jade in an ancient building or tomb, they know it most likely belonged to someone of a high status who was rich and powerful.

CHAPTER 2

Wars and armies

Before the warring states of China were united, each area had its own army. The different armies fought each other for land and to try to overthrow the ruling family so that they could form their own dynasty. After China united under one emperor, there was a much more organized army. This army was used to conquer neighbouring peoples and claim their lands. The ancient Chinese also needed weapons and defensive structures to protect themselves from their greatest enemies – the Mongol warriors who lived to the north of the kingdom.

The Terracotta Army

One of the most amazing artefacts that provides evidence about ancient Chinese soldiers is the Terracotta Army. This is an army of around 8,000 life-size soldiers made from clay. It was found buried near Emperor Qin's tomb. Each of the soldiers were made individually and they are thought to have been based on real soldiers who served in the emperor's army. The clay statues vary in height, uniform and hairstyle, in accordance with **rank**.

TERRACOTTA ARMY

A team of around 700,000 workers built the Terracotta Army over a period of about 40 years. It was discovered in 1974 by farmers who were digging a well.

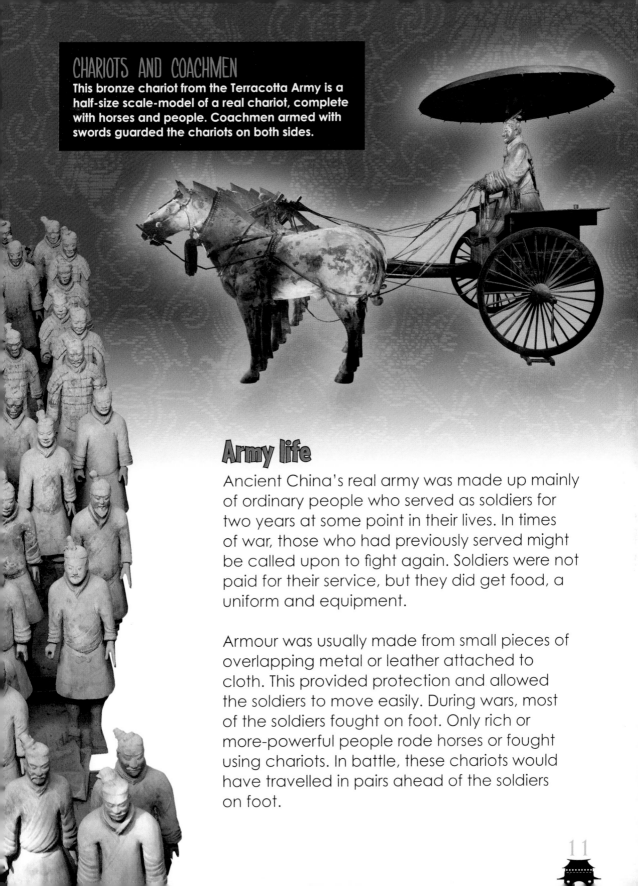

CHARIOTS AND COACHMEN

This bronze chariot from the Terracotta Army is a half-size scale-model of a real chariot, complete with horses and people. Coachmen armed with swords guarded the chariots on both sides.

Army life

Ancient China's real army was made up mainly of ordinary people who served as soldiers for two years at some point in their lives. In times of war, those who had previously served might be called upon to fight again. Soldiers were not paid for their service, but they did get food, a uniform and equipment.

Armour was usually made from small pieces of overlapping metal or leather attached to cloth. This provided protection and allowed the soldiers to move easily. During wars, most of the soldiers fought on foot. Only rich or more-powerful people rode horses or fought using chariots. In battle, these chariots would have travelled in pairs ahead of the soldiers on foot.

Weapons made for winning

Ancient Chinese warriors used a variety of weapon such as swords, spears, lances, battle-axes, shields and crossbows. These weapons were crafted with such skill that they made ancient Chinese armies a force to be reckoned with.

Pole weapons

Soldiers on foot mainly used pole weapons, such as spears and lances, which were long wooden sticks with sharpened metal or stone heads at the top. Over time, the wooden poles rotted away, but the metal and stone heads remained. The dagger-axe was the first Chinese weapon that was designed purely for war, instead of also being used for hunting. While spears had a pointed end like an arrowhead for thrusting into opponents, the dagger-axe had an L-shaped bronze blade mounted on a long pole. It was used by soldiers on chariots who would swing its long shaft to sweep and hook at the enemy. Foot soldiers usually carried a shield for protection against attack from enemy weapons such as arrows and spears.

DOUBLE-EDGED SWORDS
This bronze jian from ancient China is a double-edged straight sword.

12

The beauty of bronze

Learning how to mine and **extract** copper and tin from rock and to make bronze weapons gave the ancient Chinese a great advantage over their enemies. Bronze swords and other weapons were stronger and harder, and could easily defeat wooden and stone weapons. Bronze swords with long, sharp-edged metal blades were invaluable for fighting in **close combat**. Bronze mechanisms were also used in ancient Chinese wooden crossbows, which appeared around 4 BC. The crossbow looked like a horizontal bow and arrow, and was a very powerful weapon. It was also more efficient than the bow and arrow. It could shoot arrows a long distance and could pierce armour. The best **marksmen** could launch 10 bolts every 15 seconds from their crossbows.

DAGGER-AXE HEAD
This is a bronze dagger-axe head, often used by soldiers on chariots to attack enemy foot soldiers.

The Great Wall

During the Qin Dynasty, Emperor Qin ordered a giant wall to be built along the northern edge of the country to try to stop the Mongols from invading the newly united China. His plan was to link and extend the northern walls of the states he conquered. The wall became known as the Great Wall of China, and it can still be seen today.

Building the wall

Qin was a harsh emperor and he forced thousands of prisoners of war, criminals, soldiers and even peasants to work on the wall. There were more than 300,000 soldiers involved in its construction. The wall was built from cut stone blocks and slabs. It is actually not one wall but many different walls, which link natural barriers such as mountains and rivers. Although the wall was begun in the Qin Dynasty, its construction took hundreds of years throughout many different dynasties.

THE GREAT WALL OF CHINA
The Great Wall of China is 21,196 kilometres (13,171 miles) long and its height ranges from 5–14 metres (16–45 feet).

Features of the wall

There were gates at different points along the wall to let people in and out, mostly, it is thought, so that **merchants** could continue to buy and sell with people from regions to the north. Dotted along its length there are also high towers, used as lookout posts, with rooms below them where soldiers could sleep when not on duty. The towers were close enough together that soldiers in one tower could see the next, so they could pass signals between them.

ANALYSE THE ANCIENTS

Take a look at this section of the Great Wall. Based on the information you have learned, can you answer the questions to analyse the ancient Chinese?

1. High towers like these were used as watchtowers. Why do you think it was so important for the ancient Chinese to keep watch on the area beyond their northern borders?

2. The ancient Chinese also built fires on top of these towers. Why do you think they did this?

CHAPTER 3

Work and trade

The kind of work you did in ancient China depended on your social standing: whether you were wealthy or poor. Wealthy and middle-class people could be nobles, merchants, politicians or work for the emperor. Some people worked as artists and craftsmen. The poorest people were peasant farmers and labourers.

The life of a farmer

Most people in ancient China were poor and were farmers. They did not farm their own land. Instead, they farmed land owned by a king or lord, one of the noble classes. They also had to give the owner of their land some of their crops as a tax to the emperor. Every year, they had to leave their farms and work for around a month for the government, either in the army or building the canals, the Great Wall or extravagant palaces.

FARMING TERRACES
Parts of China are very dry or mountainous, so digging terraces like these for growing rice increased the area of land for farming and the amount of rice that could be grown.

Growing crops

Farmers in northern China, where it was cooler and drier, tended to grow cereal crops such as millet. Millet was boiled to make a type of porridge. The main crop in most of China was rice, particularly in the south where more rain fell. Farmers worked hard and harvested two or three rice crops a year.

Tools of the trade

Rice plants grow best with their roots underwater, so rice farmers dug rice terraces. These are narrow-walled fields up the sides of hills, which trapped rainwater. Fields used for growing rice are called rice paddies. In other areas, canals were dug to flood more fields throughout the country for growing rice. The ancient Chinese invented a V-shaped iron plough to help them farm. The iron head of the plough cut into the soil, then a flat iron part turned it over. They used oxen to pull the plough. This greatly increased the area of land they could prepare for planting.

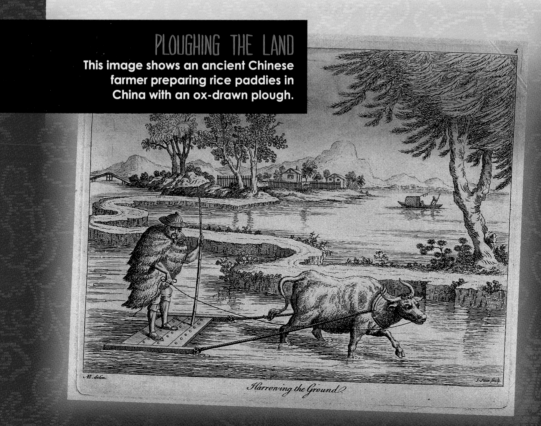

PLOUGHING THE LAND
This image shows an ancient Chinese farmer preparing rice paddies in China with an ox-drawn plough.

Merchants and makers

The ancient Chinese developed many skilled crafts, which they used to make useful objects. They made decorations for buildings and goods to sell.

Secrets of silk

According to a Chinese legend, Chinese **Empress** Xi Ling Shi discovered silk when a silkworm cocoon fell into her cup of tea. She lived in a palace with a garden with many mulberry trees. Silkworm larvae feed on mulberry leaves, then spin silk thread cocoons around themselves when they are ready to transform into moths. The Chinese learned to remove the threads and spin them together to make silk fabric. The Chinese kept silk-making a closely guarded secret for hundreds of years. There was a law that threatened death by torture to anyone who revealed it. This ensured that silk became a precious and highly sought-after fabric in other countries.

SILKEN TREASURES
This piece of delicate, cloud-patterned silk was found in an ancient Chinese tomb. It dates back to the Han Dynasty.

Lacquer

Lacquer objects were also expensive and prized. Lacquerware was an art form unique to ancient China. To make lacquerware objects, workers made a type of varnish from the **sap** of the lacquer tree. They added red or black colouring to the lacquer, then applied it to wood or bamboo objects such as boxes, music boxes and coffins. As the lacquer dried, it set. Lacquer objects were valued because they were time-consuming to create. It may have taken six coats of lacquer to coat one cup.

Porcelain

Another important invention was a fine, delicate type of pottery known as porcelain, which can be so thin it is almost transparent, or see-through. It was used to create cups, plates and other useful items for decoration or gifts. Porcelain was also used to create decorative statues and trinkets for the higher classes. The Chinese were the sole producers of such porcelain in the ancient world.

Money and trade

The ancient Chinese traded goods up and down the country for many years. Then, during the Han Dynasty, they also started trading with other countries. A network of trade routes developed along a road on which traders and merchants carried goods for sale in and out of the country.

The clues in the coins

Cowrie shells were used as **currency** in the late Xia and the Shang dynasties. Cowrie shells were rare, so the amount of money available was limited. People started to make bronze replicas of cowries, which were used before the first Chinese coins. These coins were cast in various shapes, such as swords and spades, during the Zhou Dynasty. During the Qin Dynasty, a single type of bronze coin was used across China. It was round with a square hole in the middle. This symbolized the union of heaven (round) and Earth (square). These coins made trade easier because everyone in the country used the same money. The coins could be strung together so they were easy to carry around. During the Han Dynasty, the coins were given different weights and values.

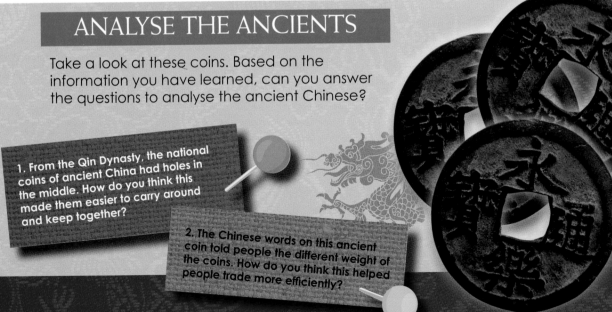

ANALYSE THE ANCIENTS

Take a look at these coins. Based on the information you have learned, can you answer the questions to analyse the ancient Chinese?

1. From the Qin Dynasty, the national coins of ancient China had holes in the middle. How do you think this made them easier to carry around and keep together?

2. The Chinese words on this ancient coin told people the different weight of the coins. How do you think this helped people trade more efficiently?

STORING GRAIN
These are the ruins of a Han Dynasty grain store, which was an important supply centre for the ancient silk routes.

The Silk Road

The ancient Chinese also traded with countries beyond China's borders. Traders carried silk, spices, tea, porcelain and other goods to the rest of Asia and to the West. They carried goods in boats called junks. They also used groups of camels, called caravans, to carry goods along the trade route from China to the West. This route became known as the Silk Road, because silk was the most valuable product that the ancient Chinese sold to the West.

CHAPTER 4

Beliefs and rituals

During the Bronze Age of China, most people worshipped hundreds of different gods and **spirits**. They also believed that when people died they passed into the spirit world too.

Many gods

The ancient Chinese believed in nature spirits, who lived in trees or streams, and each town, village, city, field and farm had its own spirit too. All of these gods or spirits were recognized and honoured. The Chinese believed they created the world and the people in it, and were still responsible for everything good and bad that happened. Each god and spirit had its own special area of power; for example, there was a god of lightning and a god of the Moon. The most important gods were given their own **shrines** and **temples**.

GUARDIANS OF DAY AND NIGHT
These spirits with animal heads and wearing Chinese robes are believed to be guardian spirits of day and night. They were painted on ceramic tiles during the Han Dynasty.

CONFUCIUS

Confucius was China's most famous teacher. He was born in 551 BC and died in 479 BC, leaving China with ideas about how to live that have lasted for centuries.

Later beliefs

After the Bronze Age, three new belief systems were introduced. Taoists believed in many different gods and that people should not interfere with nature. They chanted religious texts, practised fortune-telling and used **meditation**. Most Taoists were nobles.

Later, the ideas of Confucius (551–479 BC) had a great influence on ancient Chinese beliefs. Confucius taught that people could live in peace if they showed respect for others and carried out their duties to their families as they should. He also encouraged the practice of ancestor worship, in which people pray and give offerings to deceased relatives.

By the end of the Han Dynasty, Buddhism, which originated in India, spread to China by the Buddhist monks who travelled along the Silk Road. Buddhism encourages followers to give up self-interest. Buddhists also practise meditation and encourage people to be truthful, honest, kind and fair.

The afterlife

The ancient Chinese believed that when people died, they passed into the spirit world. This meant that life carried on after death. They also believed that people continued to do things in the **afterlife** that they did during their life on Earth. For this reason, they were careful to bury their loved ones with objects they thought they would need to take with them, from useful things such as cooking pots to personal possessions such as jewellery. They often used designs that they believed could frighten evil spirits and provide a link between the people on Earth and the gods.

V.I.P. BURIAL

This jade burial suit was made to completely cover the body of an important person. The jade helped preserve the body. More than 2,000 plates of jade were used to make it and they are held together with gold and silver wire.

This object is called a yun and it was used in ancient China to offer wine to the dead during ancestral worship ceremonies. Read the information on these pages about the ancient Chinese belief in the afterlife, then use it to answer the questions about why this object looks as it does.

1. It took a lot of skill to make this beautifully decorated bronze wine jug. Why do you think the ancient Chinese used wine jugs to make offerings to ancestors and why do you think they made them so beautiful and valuable?

2. The symbol on this yun is the taotie, known as the demon-face or the face of a sacrificial animal. Why do you think they put a figure like this on the pot?

Burial gifts

Rich and powerful people made extravagant plans for their own burials. They planned to be buried with many precious objects to define their status in the next life. They were often buried with items carved or cut from jade. The ancient Chinese believed that jade had magical powers and could protect the dead from evil spirits.

Worshipping ancestors

The ancient Chinese believed that when people died and lived on in the spirit world, they could communicate with the gods there and even influence the gods to bring good or bad luck to the people left on Earth. While on Earth, they made offerings of food to help them survive in the afterlife. They also held ceremonies to keep their ancestors happy and to persuade them to bring good luck. They feared that if they displeased or neglected their ancestors, the ancestors would bring them bad fortune. Neglected ancestors could become "hungry ghosts" who could be very vengeful and dangerous.

Predicting the future

The ancient Chinese also believed they could tell the future. Emperors and members of the royal court used **oracle bones** to predict what would happen and what they should do. The earliest oracle bones ever found are about 3,000 years old and believed to have been used by the court of the Shang Dynasty.

How oracle bones worked

Oracle bones were often made from the shoulder blade of an ox, but bones from other animals such as horses, pigs and deer were also used, as well as the undersides of tortoise shells. Once the bone had been carefully sawn to shape, shallow pits were drilled on one side of the bone. Then an official would write in red ink or engrave a question onto it on behalf of the ruling family. Next, heat was applied to the hollow pits with hot metal spikes. The heat caused the bones to crack and **priests** interpreted the patterns of the cracks to answer the questions.

ORACLE BONES
Oracle bones were used by priests in the service of the ruler.

Why oracle bones matter

The questions written on the oracle bones tell us a lot about what was important to ancient Chinese emperors. Questions ranged from what crops to plant and what the weather was going to be like to the right time to go to war or fight a battle, and the correct way to perform certain rituals. Questions about weather forecasts may seem silly to us, but they show how important it was to have good harvests to feed the people so that the dynasty remained stable and was successful. Oracle bones are also important because they are the earliest records we have of Chinese writing. Some of the characters found on these bones are still in use – and virtually unchanged – today.

FINDING ORACLE BONES

Oracle bones found in tombs like this one, of the Shang royal wife Fu Hao, tell us which gods and spirits they recognized, and which ancestors they worshipped.

CHAPTER 5

Inventions

The ancient Chinese made great advances in science and technology, and came up with several important inventions that have had a lasting impact on the world.

Paper

The invention of paper greatly contributed to the spread and development of the Chinese and later other civilizations. Before paper, the ancient Chinese used bones, tortoise shells, bamboo and other wood to write on and make books, but these were bulky and heavy to carry around. A court official named Cai Lun is believed to have invented the first paper in about AD 10 during the Han Dynasty. He came up with the idea of making sheets of paper from the bark of trees, hemp fabric waste, old rags and fishnets, which he soaked in water and mashed up. The mash was then flattened into sheets and dried.

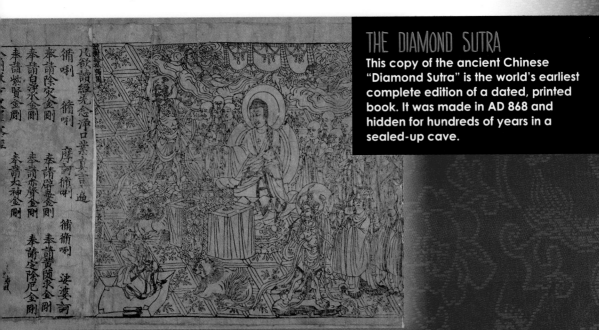

THE DIAMOND SUTRA

This copy of the ancient Chinese "Diamond Sutra" is the world's earliest complete edition of a dated, printed book. It was made in AD 868 and hidden for hundreds of years in a sealed-up cave.

Printing

The ancient Chinese came up with another important invention that helped spread information and knowledge: woodblock printing. Woodblock printing is a method in which text, images or patterns are carved into blocks of wood that are then dipped in ink and printed on fabric or paper. The printing press was a very useful invention, because it meant many copies could be made quickly, where once they were copied out individually by hand, which was very time-consuming. In Asia, woodblock printing remained the most common method of printing texts and images until the 19th century. Printing helped to spread Buddhism because Buddhist monks printed Buddhist texts using woodblocks and then distributed them.

Kites

Paper was used in another interesting way to send signals and messages in ancient China: as paper kites. The first kites were invented during the Warring States period. They were made of light wood and cloth, and later from paper. Soldiers used kites to measure distances and to calculate wind speed and direction. They also used kites to send signals on the battlefield, rather like the way ships send signals with flags at sea.

KITES
Kite flying is still popular in China today.

From mistakes to machines

Some ancient Chinese inventions were discovered by mistake. Others were made by inventors working long and hard over their ideas. Gunpowder was invented accidentally when scientists working for the emperor were told to make him a potion that would make him immortal so he would never die. One mixture of substances they tried suddenly exploded when they heated it. They first used gunpowder to make fireworks, then used it in war to scare enemies. Later, they used it in battle as a kind of explosive.

The compass

A compass is an instrument that shows directions. It was invented by the ancient Chinese during the Warring States period. This early compass was a ladle-like piece of lodestone rock, which is magnetic, sitting on a bronze plate. The handle of the ladle points south, while the other end points north.

NAVIGATION TOOL
The compass greatly improved a ship's ability to navigate over long distances.

A super seismograph

Earthquakes were a big problem in ancient China. There were many earthquakes and they were often strong. According to court records from the Han Dynasty, Zhang Heng invented the first seismograph (a machine to detect earthquakes) in AD 132. His seismograph was used to tell when, and in what direction, an earthquake happened from hundreds of kilometres away. It was a bronze jar about 1 metre (3 feet) across, surrounded by eight small dragons and eight small frogs, all with open mouths. The dragons' mouths each held a ball that would drop into the mouth of the frog below it to show which direction the earthquake was coming from.

ANALYSE THE ANCIENTS

Using information you have learned about ancient Chinese inventions, answer the questions about how this seismograph works.

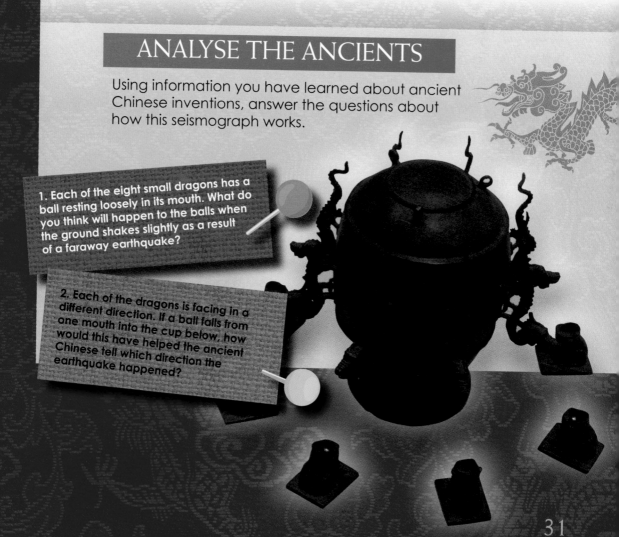

1. Each of the eight small dragons has a ball resting loosely in its mouth. What do you think will happen to the balls when the ground shakes slightly as a result of a faraway earthquake?

2. Each of the dragons is facing in a different direction. If a ball falls from one mouth into the cup below, how would this have helped the ancient Chinese tell which direction the earthquake happened?

Chinese medicine

Many people in ancient China believed that sickness, pain and disease were caused by demons or curses, or that they happened because they had displeased their gods or ancestors in some way. They tried to cure themselves by chanting spells or eating what they believed were dragon bones, which were probably in fact the **fossils** of ordinary animal bones. However, the ancient Chinese also invented new medical treatments that really worked, some of which are still used today.

Herbal medicines

After tasting and testing different plants, the ancient Chinese developed many medicines. Herbal medicine was used in teas to cure common illnesses such as colds, flus, coughs, stomach aches and diarrhoea. Herbal medicines were made from many different plants, such as ginger, ginseng, liquorice and garlic. They were often dried, crushed into a powder, then added to boiling water and dissolved. The patient then drank the medicine like a cup of tea.

CHINESE HERBS
Herbal medicines have been used since 3 BC. Many people still use them today.

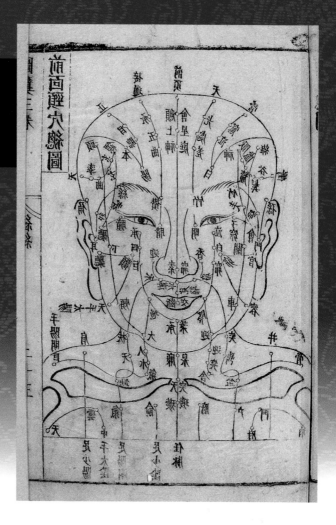

Acupuncture

The ancient Chinese started using acupuncture around 2500 BC and it is still used today. Acupuncture is the practice of inserting small, fine metal needles in the skin and leaving them in position for around 30 minutes. The needles are placed somewhere along 12 pathways in the body, called meridians, each one of which is linked to a different body part. Acupuncturists believe that the human body's life force follows these lines and that by stimulating them, illnesses can be improved and pain eased. Men who knew how to use acupuncture needles taught their sons, but the secret of this treatment was kept in healers' families alone for many centuries. Acupuncture is still known to be effective in relieving pain, and is used in China today as an anaesthetic to put people to sleep during surgery.

CHAPTER 6

Everyday life

In ancient China, your position in society was mostly defined by the family into which you were born. If you were born into a peasant farming family, you would become a farmer too.

The great divide

There was a great divide between the everyday lives of the ruling classes, nobles, wealthy traders and business owners, and the peasant farmers and labourers who worked for them. The only way to move up in the world was to pass a difficult test and get a job as an official working for the government. However, only those who could read could study for the test, and only the rich could afford books and education. There were even separate drinking and eating places for rich men and poor men to go to after work – the lower classes were not allowed near the places of higher-class men.

HAIRPINS FOR THE RICH

Valuable and decorative hairpins like this would only have been worn by the very wealthy, the nobles or the royal family.

This painting on silk was found draped over the coffin of a powerful woman from the Han Dynasty. It shows the layers of heaven, Earth and the underworld that the ancient Chinese believed in.

Different clothes

The clothes people wore in ancient China immediately showed others their status. Only nobles and royalty were allowed to wear silk. Even the merchants who sold it were not allowed to wear it. There were rules about what colours people wore and those who disobeyed could be punished. Emperors wore colourful silks and different dynasties chose different colours to represent them. Their long robes were covered in detailed embroidery in designs ranging from dragons to clouds. Jewellery, such as hairpins, made from ivory, silver or gold also showed a person's rank.

Most people wore drab-coloured and loose-fitting clothing made of plant fibres, such as hemp or ramie, which is a nettle-like plant. They wore simple tunics, trousers and thick, padded jackets in winter for warmth. One common thing the rich and poor shared was that they all had long hair. Only criminals had short hair because it was cut off as part of their punishment.

Palaces and huts

Rich people and the emperor's family lived in grand houses and palaces, and poor people lived in what we would describe today as little more than huts. However, the way of laying out a house and the materials used to build them were similar.

Home sweet home

Most settlements were placed within the protective folds of mountains, where they were shielded from strong winds. Houses were built on **foundations** of **compressed** earth mixed with sand, gravel or clay. The walls were built of wood, brick or mud, and tiles were often used for roofs. In the south, people also used bamboo to build. Rich and poor homes were laid out in a similar way. There was a central rectangular courtyard with a garden. Poor people would build several huts around a shared courtyard. The rich had separate rooms for sleeping, eating and cooking, as well as a large hall for entertaining that was connected to the courtyard. The poor would often use movable folding screens to divide up their living space. All kitchens included a shrine for the kitchen god.

CHINESE PALACES
This is a pottery model of an ancient Chinese palace.

Furnishings

Most homes had very little furniture, but they usually had a kang bed, especially in the cooler north of China. The kang was a long, raised platform made of bricks or clay with a space beneath to build a fire. People often sat here to eat and, in poorer homes, this also acted as the sitting area in the daytime. Rich people had more furniture, which was highly decorated to show off their wealth. The hall, where guests were received, held the most expensive furniture.

Grand palaces

Palaces were often large with a completely enclosed courtyard for privacy and to prevent thieves from seeing the wealth within. Palace complexes also had temples and towers, and some palaces had moats as well as high walls to keep the poor separate from the rich. The palaces were filled with decorative objects made from bronze or gold, such as oil lamps, statues and porcelain vases and pots.

Feasts and food

The main food that people in ancient China ate, whether they were rich or poor, was rice. Most people ate rice at every meal. Some people ate noodles, which were also invented in China. They were made from wheat, millet or rice. People cooked using chopsticks, which early emperors had made from elephant tusks. They first used chopsticks to reach deep into boiling pots of water or oil to stir food. Later, they began to use chopsticks to eat.

Rich and poor

Most people ate their rice or millet with vegetables. This was partly because those foods were cheaper and easier to get. It may also have been because the Chinese temples and **monasteries** taught people that vegetarianism was healthy and a way to be kind to animals. Families often kept chickens for their eggs. If people lived near rivers, they caught and ate fish too. In some places, they used birds, such as cormorants, to catch the fish for them. The birds had rings around their throats to stop them from swallowing the fish that they caught. Emperors and their families ate more meat, such as pork, beef and even horse. They had teams of chefs and servants working for them, who also prepared pheasant, roasted duck, wild boar and bear paws for royal families at feasts and festival times.

COOKING MEALS
The image on this tile found in an ancient Chinese tomb shows a meal being prepared in a home.

Home cooking

People in ancient China cooked their food over a fire in a three-legged pot known as a ding. The pot sat over the fire and bubbled slowly all day, so a meal was ready for the family when it came in from the fields. People drank water or tea with their meals – tea was another Chinese invention. Tea was first brewed in about 2700 BC by pouring boiling water over dried and powdered leaves of the camellia plant. This tea was a kind of medicine that people believed would keep them healthy, but it was also a popular drink that people enjoyed.

Family life

The home was the centre of family life. Women took care of the home, while men worked outside. Peasant children worked with their parents. Boys from wealthy homes went to school, while girls stayed at home learning skills for how to tend to the home. The emperor's family members did nothing. Servants did everything for them and even fed them. They grew their fingernails very long to prove how rich and important they were.

BANQUETS FOR THE EMPEROR
This painting shows servants waiting on an emperor's officials during an outdoor banquet.

Read the information on this page about the popular ancient Chinese board game called Weichi, and see if you can then answer these questions.

1. The board game Weichi is laid out with a grid of squares, and players put one stone down at a time and try to surround the other's pieces. How do you think this relates to the way generals used to plan their attacks?

2. This game could be played with pieces as simple as black stones and white stones. How do you think that helped make it popular with many different kinds of people?

Entertainment

Outdoor games enjoyed by the ancient Chinese included kickball, football, wrestling and archery. After eating, families talked and played games at home, and young children might play with a pet cat. They enjoyed playing games together, such as mah-jong or draughts. The oldest board game was called Weichi, or Go, and it was invented in ancient China more than 2,500 years ago. In English, Weichi means "surrounding game", and the aim is to surround more territory than your opponent. Many people think that the game developed from the way Chinese generals used stones to map out attacking positions. The game was played by putting black stones and white stones on a wooden board painted with lines that formed squares.

A mighty civilization

As with previous dynasties, many innovations were developed during the final dynasty of ancient Chinese times – the Han Dynasty. As well as inventing paper and opening up the Silk Road, people started to use pulleys and wheelbarrows to move goods during the Han Dynasty. They used water-powered hammers to crush grains, and bellows to pump air into furnace fires that helped them make metal goods. Yet one of the things that made the ancient Chinese so great, and that tells us so much about them today, was their writing.

History in words

Early Chinese writing took the form of picture symbols, but gradually China's system of writing became standardized and more complex, with thousands of different characters. The wide range of written records left by the Chinese in various forms, from tomb inscriptions, oracle stones, laws and books, provides us with the evidence for much of what we know about their history. Chinese writing was very important in ancient China for uniting the ancient Chinese people, and for spreading and sharing information so they could make further advances. No wonder the most important art form in ancient China was calligraphy – the art of beautiful handwriting.

GEAR WHEELS

This is a Han Dynasty mould used for making bronze gear wheels. Waterwheels were used to turn gears to lift and drop hammers that crushed grains to make flour.

This bronze sculpture of the Flying Horse of Gansu has become a symbol of China. It was found in a tomb from the Han Dynasty. It represents an ideal horse that can gallop so fast it can outrun the wind.

Times of change

The Han Dynasty ended in AD 220. It had been in trouble for a while, after a period of many natural disasters. People thought it was a sign the gods were unhappy with their leaders. Also, one Han emperor after another had died young or without an **heir**. Then, in AD 190, a **warlord** named Dong Zhou took control of the empire. He turned a child from the Han family into emperor, but Zhou controlled the country. By AD 220, the emperor was gone and the Han Dynasty was over. The country was then torn apart by wars between states. Although it was the end of the great dynasty age, ancient China gave birth to a modern country that is just as fascinating and vibrant.

ANSWERS

Did you manage to analyse the ancients? Check your answers against the correct answers on these pages.

PAGE 9

1. In ancient China, jade was a precious and rare stone that was very expensive. People who had items made from it or buried with them in their tombs were usually rich and powerful.

2. Rich and powerful people chose the dragon symbol because it represented power and strength.

PAGE 15

1. Soldiers in watchtowers were on the lookout for Mongols from the north. The Mongols were China's greatest enemy and the Chinese feared attack by these fierce warriors.

2. When a guard lit a fire in one watchtower, this told the guard in the next tower that there was danger. The second guard would light a fire too. One after the other, fires were lit to pass the message down the line that China was in imminent danger and invasion was likely.

PAGE 20

1. The square central hole allows the coins to be conveniently and safely strung together.

2. Different weights had different values so they could be used to buy and sell different things.

PAGE 25

1. Using beautiful bronze vessels showed honour and respect to the ancestors being worshipped and kept them happy. People believed that if you did not show the proper respect to ancestors, they would be displeased and would stop helping them and keeping them safe. People gave their ancestors drinks such as wine in the hope they would keep them safe.

2. The Chinese believed that the design of offering vessels, like the one on page 25, could send a message to the gods and frighten demons. The demon figure could frighten evil spirits and provide a link between people on Earth and the gods.

PAGE 31

1. The balls in the seismograph sat lightly in the dragons' mouths so they fell out easily if there was even a slight shaking of the ground as a result of an earthquake.

2. The dragons face in different directions so that even if someone was out of the room when a ball fell, they could still tell which direction the earthquake happened by seeing which cup it fell into.

PAGE 41

1. It is said that generals used boards like the one shown on page 41 to lay out their plan of attack before a battle.

2. The game did not involve money but was played using stones. Therefore it could be enjoyed by anyone.

GLOSSARY

afterlife life after death

artefacts objects from the past that tell us about people's lives

bronze a metal made from a mixture of tin and copper, which are metals found in rock

civilization a settled community in which people live together peacefully and use systems such as writing to communicate

close combat fighting opponents at short range

compressed packed together

culture the beliefs, customs and arts of a group of people or a country

currency the type of money that a country uses

dynasties families that rule a country for a long time by passing control from father to son

emperor a male ruler or king

empress a female ruler or queen

extract to remove

fossils the remains of a plant or an animal that lived millions of years ago

foundations the solid structure that supports a building from beneath

heir a person who inherits a title

jade a hard, usually green stone

marksmen people skilled at shooting

meditation to focus completely on one's thoughts or religion

merchants people who buy and sell goods

monasteries buildings in which monks live

mythical something imaginary or invented that does not really exist

oracle bones objects used in ancient China to predict the future

priests religious leaders

rank position of importance in an army or other group

rituals religious ceremonies

sap a sticky fluid found beneath the bark of a tree

shrines places for worship that are smaller than temples

spirits supernatural beings

symbols images that represent something else

taxes regular payments people make to their ruler or government to help run a country

temples buildings where people go to worship their god or gods

tomb a building where dead people are put to rest

warlord a leader of a military group who is not part of a government and who fights against other leaders

Books

Ancient China (You Choose: Historical Eras), Terry Lee Collins (Raintree, 2015)

Daily Life in Shang Dynasty China (Daily Life in Ancient Civilizations), Lori Hile (Raintree, 2016)

Shang Dynasty China (Great Civilisations), Tracey Kelly (Franklin Watts, 2016)

The Shang Dynasty of Ancient China (The History Detective Investigates), Geoff Barker (Wayland, 2015)

Websites

Find out about the ancient Shang Dynasty at:
www.bbc.co.uk/bitesize/topics/z39j2hv

Learn more about ancient China at:
www.dkfindout.com/us/history/ancient-china

Discover a lot of fun facts about ancient China at:
www.ducksters.com/history/china/ancient_china.php

Find out more about ancient China at:
www.historyforkids.net/ancient-china.html

INDEX